THE

NEW

BACHELOR'S

COOKBOOK

❖ ❖ ❖

by

Henri C. Marsh, D.V.M.

❖ ❖ ❖

"A gift of CARING "

from_____, because I CARE!

R&E Publishers
P.O. Box 2008, Saratoga, CA 95070
Tel: (408) 866-6303   Fax: (408) 866-0825

Book Design and Typesetting by Cathy Ortelle

Cover by Kaye Quinn

Library of Congress Card Catalog Number: 92-56392

ISBN 0-88247-955-5

Designed, typeset and totally manufactured in the
United States of America

dedication

. . . To the new guy in the kitchen with the hope that he will preserve his sense of perspective, his sense of self worth, his sense of balance, and perhaps most important of all—preserve his sense of humor!

. . . To the good friend of the new guy in the kitchen, who CARED enough . . . . .

acknowledgements

- or -
Many Thanks to ALL -
For ALL of Your Contributions!

Every single person listed in this book is forever etched in the kudos of this undertaking, for what is a cookbook without recipes? To each of you goes not only my culinary heartfelt thanks, but sincere thanks as well from all of the bachelor cooks who will enjoy your recipes through the use of this book.

Very special thanks go to Audrey Christie who offered me my very first recipe, not for this book but for my "palatal" salvation. Madalyn Pollock and Kay Elman offered to proofread my manuscript - little did they know how many revisions there would be, but I never heard a complaint from either lady! (And more than anyone else, Kay "shaped up" my manuscript when it really needed it!) Without them, this undertaking would still be a figment of my imagination. Special thanks also to Mary Mason Hull for her encouragement and friendly-frequent question—"Is your cookbook completed - YET?"

I'll let you in on a little secret—I always knew I had a "special" recipe when its creator could recite it from memory without any hesitancy!

Last (and maybe least!) I must thank my "exes," for without them, I would never have been a NEW BACHELOR—and would have had no reason to conceive or write this book!

time out!

For its merit I will knight it,
*   and then it will be Sir-loin.*
. . . Charles II, to a fine cut of beef!

We may live without friends;
*   we may live without books;*
But civilized man cannot live
*   without cooks!*
*   . . . Owen Meredith*

The only premarital thing girls
don't do these days is cooking!
*   . . . Omar Sharif*

I would like to find a stew
that will give me heartburn
immediately, instead of at three
o'clock in the morning.
*   . . . John Barrymore*

Serenely full, the epicure
*   would say,*
Fate cannot harm me—
*   I have dined today!*
*   . . . Sydney Smith*

Other men lived to eat,
*   while he ate to live.*
*   . . . Socrates*

To eat is human, to digest, divine!
*   . . . Mark Twain*

contents

A word about TOMATOES 3
Italian tomato sauce............................. 4
Henry's delicious manicotti 6
Baked chicken 7
Hints on freezing.................................. 7
Easy hors d'oerves 8
Time out! 9
French onion soup 9
Cleaning hints 10
Time out! 11
Quiche 12
Time out! 13
"Season to taste" 13
Salmon filet dijonaise 14
Fran's speedy turkey loaf 15
Microwave vegetables 16
Salad dressing supreme 17
Split pea soup 18
Baked beans,southern style 19
If you hate SPINACH 20
Wok cooking 21
Baked carrots 23
Time out 24
Pot roast delicioso 25
Pecan cheese ball 25

A lesson in Breast Anatomy 26
Chicken divan extraordinare 27
Time out 28
Eggplant soup 29
Johnny Carson says 30
A party dip that's a snap! 30
Oriental squash,delicio! 31
"O" chicken shish-kabob 32
Easy as pie,that's a pie! 33
End of month meal 34
A time out! 34
A new slant on a baked potato 35
Time out! 35
Marinara sauce ala suglia 36
Time out! 37
Meet my new friend,"Suzi" 37
Spaghetti sauce"by the two's" 38
One dish colorful pasta delight 40
Time out! 41
Fettucini 42
A jogger's (Harvard) hamburger 42
London broil 43
My Susan's simple savory supper 43
Susie's cheesecake 44
Tasty eggplant parmesan 45
Time out! 46
Orange cinnamon french toast 47
Meatballs, by Joyce! 48
Sauce, by Joyce! 49
Time out! 50
Kitchen equipment 51
Time out! 53
Ratatouille vitrier 54
A "hull" of a chicken! 56
Tomato soup ala ambrosia 57

From the "tip" of the Hull 58
A word about eggs 59
Garlic sticks 59
Time out! 60
Gabriella's great chicken delight 61
Salad by Mary 62
Straight from heaven Hawiian cake 63
Mashed potatoes 64
Peanut brittle 64
Walnut chopped "liver" 65
Time out! 66
Coconut pie ala Elman! 67
Time out! 68
Wackie cake,by Mary! 69
Bulgarian eggpant dip 70
Pasta with garlic 71
Garbanzo bean dip 72
Joni's beer bread 72
12 bean soup 73
Super Kay's super Scotch scones 74
Kay's souffle! 75
Time out! 76
Consider 76
Spicy Kay's chili chowder! 77
Kay's—sassy, spicy chicken 78
Potato salad-by Goring! 79
Time out! 80
Steamed marinated chicken 81
Time out! 82
Gloria's apple cake—by Mary! 83
Kay's quickie tidbit! 84
Non-fat chocolate syrup!!! 85
Time out! 85
Spinach Dip 86
Dijon Vinaigrette 86

Low-cal Tuna or Crab Dip.......................87
Deviled Dip...87
Curry Dip 88
"Counter-culture" Cornell bread 89
Chicken soup 91
Citrus candy..92
Consider 93
Last word!! 94
AND...ONE MORE LAST WORD!! 94

COOKBOOK

FOR

NEW BACHELORS

This is not a sexist book (maybe sexy a bit, as we get going), but the title indicates my belief that new bachelorettes are much more conversant and comfortable with cook books, kitchens, ovens, shopping, menus, refrigeration of foods, etc. than we bachelors. So, this book is intended for the new guy in the kitchen as I found myself one day, hardly knowing how to boil water, let alone how to make a roux, or know the meaning of saute', flambe', or even flan.

It is not the intention of the author to make a gourmet cook out of you, but merely to keep you alive for a few months during the (probably) most stressful days of your life. I am not a nutritionist, nor a psychologist/psychiatrist—just a veterinarian with a bit (I hope) of . . . horse sense!

I was literally afraid of a kitchen and was convinced that the art of cooking was similar to duplicating a drug prescription—there could be no room for error or 'free thinking'. I have found that this is definitely NOT the case with cooking. Roll up your sleeves, put a smile on your face, and have some fun. If you goof up once in a while, you can always call out for pizza or Chinese! (Or use it up by sending it over to your EX . . . in a doggy bag!) So loosen up - you're under enough pressure right now - and show the old lady that you can damn well do it, too! Good Luck!

If you don't have an elevated cholesterol or high blood pressure problem - eat now as though you do! Saturated fats are found in most animal fats, in chocolate (not cocoa), in coconuts and in fats often used in processed foods—the so-called tropical fats, coconut and palm, and hydrogenated vegetable oils. These fats stimulate the cholesterol-making cells in your liver, raising your blood-cholesterol level, and, in turn, your risk of heart attack and stroke. So it makes very good sense to cut out fried foods, most animal fats, hard cheeses, whole milk and cream. The experts recommend that we consume no more than 10% of our calories as saturated fat - that's a third less than what government food surveys say we're eating now. There is an honest difference of opinion within the medical/nutritional communities concerning the use of butter vs. margarine. Margarine, although containing no cholesterol, does apparently contain something almost or just as bad, called "trans fats," which are put there by the manufacturing process. You should know that the more solid margarines contain more trans fats, so it is best to use margarine packaged in tubs rather than in sticks.

I have used butter and margarine interchangeably in this book, but my "horse sense" tells me to use either one sparingly! Get in the habit, for example, of using only jellies or jams on toast! I'll get into little secrets which will tell you how to replace those tastes, but right now, let's get into some recipes!

To begin: I have tried all of these recipes myself—they are easy to do, taste good, are nutritious, and most can be put in small containers and frozen, to be warmed up later in the month.

time out!

. . . *"There is no love sincerer than the love of food."*
. . . . *George Bernard Shaw*

. . . *"The most dangerous food a man can eat is wedding cake."*
. . . . *American Proverb*

. . . *"Kissing don't last; cookery do!"* . . . . *George Meredith*

. . .a word about TOMATOES. . .

Until about 1840, the tomato was considered a poisonous plant because it belongs to the same family, botanically, as deadly nightshade (i.e. belladonna) . . .

Botanically, the tomato is the ripened ovary of a seed plant - that makes it a fruit. But in 1893, it took the U.S. Supreme Court to decide that the tomato was not a fruit but a vegetable (Tariff Act, 1883) . . .

The tomato is the favorite homegrown crop of American backyard gardeners - 85% of the 30 million home gardeners grow them! . . .

Except for the potato, the tomato is America's most important commercial vegetable both in weight consumed (nine million tons plus, annually) and annual yield (more than $1.4 billion!).

italian tomato sauce

Here's the one recipe that can be used with such versa-
tility that it can truly be a lifesaver. Cover any pasta with
it - from vermicelli (I prefer this to spaghetti - the diameter
is smaller, thus absorbing more sauce!), to pasta shells,
to covering most any vegetable, etc. You can use your
imagination with this one.

Ingredients:

2 small onions
(or one large)
2 green peppers
2 cloves of fresh
garlic, peeled -
get the old flaky
stuff off. Then,
lay a wide-
blade kitchen
knife flatways
on the clove and
hit the knife
with the heel of
your hand to
crush the garlic.
Mince (chop up
rather finely).

Use a large pot, and cover the
bottom with olive oil. Chop above
ingredients and cook on low heat
until the onions are transparent,
not brown. (About 20 minutes.)
Remove from pot and place in bowl
for later use.

In same pot, drop 1 or 2 large,
lean pork chops - 1/2" thick. (two
thick lamb chops or chicken breasts
works well, too) Cook again for about
10 minutes on each side, less for
chicken breasts, or until both sides
are brown. (You probably will need
a little more olive oil in the pot.)

(continued)

Add:

2 cans whole
   peeled tomatoes
   (dog food size
   cans). Squeeze
   tomatoes to
   break up a bit.
2 same size cans
   of Spanish
   tomato sauce (if
   you can't find
   the Spanish,
   use any of them)
1 teaspoonful salt
4 teaspoonfuls
   pepper
4 teaspoonfuls
   oregano
4 teaspoonfuls
   basil
4 teaspoonfuls
   parsley, dried or
   fresh-minced

Add the cooked onions, garlic and fresh green pepper. Stir well, and put pot <u>uncovered</u> in the oven set at 250° for six to seven hours. Stir occasionally if you're home. Whatever meat you have used - pork, lamb or chicken - usually breaks up during the cooking process, but sometimes I find I must cut it up some; or, sometimes I will enjoy the first meal from this recipe using this meat as the meat course for my dinner! Sometimes I make this up in the morning and stick it in the oven just before I leave home for the office. Hint: When I make this recipe, I generally double all the ingredients - it's just as easy to cook a full pot as a half pot! This recipe freezes very well. Let it cool a bit before packaging it for freezing. See hints on freezing (page 7).

. . . this recipe was the very first given me and I owe the idea of this entire book to the lovely lady who cared: Audrey Christy (and my good friend, Jim, her husband.)

henry's delicious manicotti —

henry black,m.d., that is!

This recipe comes directly from my friend and cardiologist! Says Henry: "Not as rich or artery clogging as the regular style but just as delicious!

Ingredients:

8 Manicotti Shells (cooked as per directions on package for stuffing)
8 ounces (1% fat) cottage cheese (Sealtest is good)
4 ounces soft tofu - available at health food stores in small 4 ounce containers that keep on the shelf forever
1 tablespoonful mixed dry Italian spices

Combine cottage cheese, tofu and Italian spices and mix until smooth. Stuff the manicotti shells and place in a lightly oiled (with olive oil) casserole dish with a cover.

Set oven at 350°.

Blend an 8 ounce can of tomatoes with 1 teaspoonful of garlic to a smooth liquid. Pour over the shells. Cover and bake for 20 minutes.

Serves two quite well. Great to serve the next day.

A fresh romaine and sprout salad with a little Italian dressing goes well with this dinner!

baked chicken
—by sandy

Ingredients:

Pre-heat oven to 375°.

One 8 ounce bottle Wishbone Russian Dressing
One package dry onion soup
1/2 cup apricot preserves

Mix ingredients together and pour over pieces of chicken (your choice!). Bake for 1 hour. Turn chicken over at half time!

Easy, delicious . . and nutritious!

. . . this recipe given me by Sandy Plank, daughter of one of my favorite cousins, Regis Crocher, with whom I shared much of my youth!

hints on freezing

Try to remove all air pockets. Wrap tightly in aluminum foil, saran wrap or freezer bags. Plastic Rubbermaid containers work well, too, but NEVER use these in a microwave with tomato based food; it stains the container. If staining occurs, place in the sun for a day or two after washing well. Try soaking in bleach as a last resort, but you may not be able to get the chlorine odor out of the plastic material. If you still have a swimming pool, drop your stained plastic containers in for a day or two - the combination of sun and chlorine should clean it up! Remember this trick for your white grimy clothes - works well! Wash 'em first, then toss in the pool while still wet.

Use masking tape as a label on frozen items and write the date on it as well. It's easy to forget what you have in the freezer!

easy hors d'oerves

Ingredients:

*Fresh mushrooms,
chopped, same
quantity as
onions*

*Onion, chopped
fine, same
quantity as
mushrooms*

*Mayonnaise
(cholesterol
free!), quantity
to produce a
paste consis-
tency*

*Romano or
Parmesan
cheese*

*(Author: For a
change in pace,
you can add
Worcestershire
Sauce or
Tabasco Sauce
to this recipe,
too!)*

Use crackers, or "round bread" which is fresh bread from which circles have been punched out using either a cookie cutter - no I don't have one, either - or a small glass or cup using the brim as the cutter. Or, you can use thin-sliced bread (anything but bleached white bread which offers so little nutrition!), sliced corner to corner (making triangles.) Your option: slice away crusts, or not.

Mix the ingredients to a paste consistency and spread liberally on bread or crackers. Sprinkle the cheese on top and place on a cookie sheet (piece of aluminum foil will do), and broil. Don't place too close to the broiler because you want to cook the onions a bit. The onions will be cooked when the top just begins to turn brown.

Don't tell your guests how easy this is! It will taste as though you slaved all day. The secret is in the mayonnaise.

. . . This recipe, and many others in this book, was given to me by my true friend and colleague, Paulette Vitrier Crabtree, herself going through a divorce at the time - which gave me insight into "the other side". Neither side is much fun.

time out!

...*"Only the pure in heart can make a good soup"*
.....*Ludwig von Beethoven*

...*"The soup is never hot enough if the waiter can keep his thumb in it"*
.....*William Collier*

french onion soup

Ingredients:

1. *Two cans (dog food size) of chicken broth - Kosher best, Swansons, very good*
2. *1 medium size onion, sliced fairly thin*
3. *Lipton onion soup mix, dry (it comes two envelopes to a package; use one envelope)*
4. *Swiss Cheese (sliced very thin, and a quality brand)*
5. *Slices of toast (any bread except non-nutritious white bread)*

In a frying pan, melt a generous teaspoonful of margarine (non-cholesterol) and add the sliced onion. Cook until the onion slices are limp, not brown.

In a saucepan, add the two cans of chicken broth, the one envelope of Lipton onion soup mix and cooked sliced onions. Simmer (barely bubbling) for 30-40 minutes. Put in oven proof bowl (pyrex, etc.) and float toast on top of soup. Cover toast with slices of swiss cheese and put in a 400° oven until cheese is nicely melted. (Less than 10 minutes - you have to keep your eye on it!).

(continued)

Here's the piéce de rèsistance:

Double or triple this recipe: follow the recipe up to the point of adding the toast and cheese, put in small containers and store in freezer. When you are ready to serve the soup, heat on top of the stove or thaw in microwave oven (if you're lucky enough to have been left with one). Add the toast and cheese, and melt in oven as above. The melting of the cheese can be done in a microwave, too, but it's not quite as good as in a regular oven. (I would be less than honest, though, if I didn't tell you that, unless I'm having some impressive company, I use the microwave!)

. . . this is another creative recipe given me by dear Paulette Vitrier Crabtree.

cleaning hints

If you've burned a pan (I mean <u>really</u> burned the damn thing!), don't fret. Soak overnight in a liberal quantity of AUTOMATIC DISHWASHER DETER-GENT and water, and the next day the pot will shine. If it doesn't, you didn't use enough detergent!

. . . this helpful hint given me by my very good friend, Laurie Goring, who has a glorious book of tre- mendous hope within her!

If you've got a stub- born stain in a washable fabric (pants, shirt, etc.), don't throw it away or waste money at the dry cleaners (you've already been taken to the cleaners, haven't you?). Make up a mixture of equal parts Joy and Wisk (laundry detergent) and rub into the stain. Let it stand for a few minutes and then wash in the clothes washer. I keep a small dispenser bottle (plastic squeeze bottle that once contained ketchup) of this mixture in the laundry; it really comes in handy! Works, too!

. . . this helpful hint (I'm beginning to feel like Heloise!) was given me by a New Jersey friend, Marcy Nadel - nice lady!

time out!

Hear about the farmer who was plowing his field one day without any pants on? When asked why he was doing this he admitted that it was his wife's idea - "Yesterday" he confided, "I worked without a shirt - and ended up with a stiff neck!"

❖❖

Here's a young girl who's destined to succeed:

She visited a farm one day and wanted to buy a large watermelon.

"That's three dollars," said the farmer. "I've only got 30 cents," said the young girl. The farmer pointed to a very small watermelon in the field and said, "How about that one?"

"Okay, I'll take it," said the little girl. "But leave it on the vine. I'll be back for it in a month."

quiche —

another vitrier winner!

This recipe is loaded with the two c's - calories and cholesterol - BEWARE! *(but it's good! Author)*

Ingredients:

2 frozen pie shells
16 slices bacon
4 sweet onions
1 lb. grated Swiss
   cheese
6 Tbsp. flour
salt & pepper
   (to taste)
2 cups hot milk
6 beaten eggs

Purchase two frozen pie shells and let thaw. Transfer the shell to pyrex pie plates if you have them; if not, use the aluminum pans provided.

Preheat oven to 325°. Cook 16 slices of bacon (*Author: I use turkey bacon, less cholesterol!*) either on the stove or in a microwave oven, until crisp. Drain well using paper towels.

Thinly slice 4 small (sweet, if available) onions and saute (fry) in butter until golden but not really brown. Spread crumbled bacon and sauted onions on bottom of pie shell.

To 1 pound of grated Swiss cheese (available already grated if you prefer), add 6 tablespoonfuls flour, salt and pepper (to taste) and toss gently.

To 2 cups of very hot, but not boiled, milk slowly add 6 beaten eggs. Quickly pour into the shells with the cheese mixture. Must be done quickly because the eggs are cooking in the hot milk!

Pop in the 325° oven for 40 minutes. Freezes well!

time out!

. . . from MAE WEST . . .

. . "It's not the men in my life that counts, it's the life in my men!

. . "Too much of a good thing can be . . . . wonderful!"

"season to taste"

"Season to taste" usually refers to adding salt and/or pepper either just before serving or just before re-heating food. Now you know!

salmon filet dijonaise

Put salmon, skin side UP, in a flat dish (oven proof, such as pyrex) and pour over it a good Italian vinaigrette salad dressing. Let this soak (marinate, they call it) - turn the fish over in about 15 minutes if you think of it, and after 30 minutes or so pour off the marinade (salad dressing!). (If you're in a hurry, even 5 minutes marinating the salmon will make a difference). Turn the fish over so the skin now is on the bottom

Pre-heat the oven (that means turn it on <u>now</u>) to 375°.

Ingredients:

2 *tablespoonfuls*
   Dijon mustard
1 *teaspoonful*
   horseradish
1 *tablespoonful*
   lime or lemon
   juice - grapefruit
   juice is OK, too -
   most any citrus
   will do.

Mix the above ingredients together in a small bowl and smear over the fish generously enough so you can't see the flesh.

After smearing on the top (non-skin) side, sprinkle black pepper over the fish - freshly ground is much preferable. Treat yourself to a good pepper mill unless you were able to hang on to one.

Place, uncovered, in the oven and bake for about 10 to 12 minutes. You'll know it's done when the fish "flakes" when disturbed with a fork. Trust me, you'll know when it's done. Serve immediately with fresh parsley or dill.

this recipe is excellent for mahi mahi!
(that's Dolphin, but not the Flipper species!)

Option to previous recipe:

(continued)

After placing fish in pyrex dish, skin side down, generously splash on lemon juice, or white wine or water - or all three!. Place a dab of margarine here and there on the fish - not too much. Bake as above.

. . .these recipes given me by the only professional chef I know. I'm privileged to call him my friend, Mr. Keith McCrea.

fran's speedy turkey loaf

Microwave Meal In Itself!

Ingredients:

1. *One lb. ground turkey, raw.*
2. *One 8 ounce can tomato sauce.*
3. *Refill above can with water.*
4. *1/4 cup Bulgar (this is partially cooked whole wheat, available at most health food stores - comes as dry granules).*
5. *1/4 cup oat bran.*
6. *One large onion, chopped medium fine (I don't know what that means, either!).*
7. *Garlic powder to taste (app. 1 Tbsp.)*

Mix above ingredients well, place in a flat pyrex dish and top with any vegetables you might have laying around looking for a home (carrots, green beans, peas, broccoli, cauliflower, etc. Make it colorful; after all, you're going to eat it). Zigzag ketchup over the top; cover and cook in microwave oven for about 30 minutes.

. . .when I was born, I was blessed by being able to head up the line when sisters were handed out. I really do have the best ever created, and this is her idea of NUTRITION!! A dear and lovable mite, Fran Moran. My brother-in-law, Ed, is AOK, too.

microwave vegetables

Ingredients:

1. *Selection of most any fresh vegetable you can think of - come on now, be kind, SHE wasn't a vegetable,....was she?Really??*
2. *1 packet of low sodium chicken broth concentrate - MBT brand preferred (look for this in soup section of your supermarket)*
3. *1 or 2 table-spoonfuls of water*
4. *Butter Buds - if you haven't heard of this, it's a terrific product; comes in a small bottle in the herb area of your supermarket. You'll need about a tablespoonful, more or less*
5. *1/2 teaspoon-ful basil, more or less, that's a good start...*

Cut up the vegetables any way you want to, throw them into a pyrex dish, add above ingredients. Sprinkle the butter buds on the top. Cover with lid, or saran wrap. Microwave to your liking; I prefer mine undercooked - about 4 to 6 minutes, but the time will depend greatly on your selection of vegetables and the power of your microwave oven - experiment!

. . . this idea given me by a lovely powerhouse tiny mite by the name of Dana Foster - a noted artist; her husband, Dick, is a successful hobby fisherman, (lucky, too!)

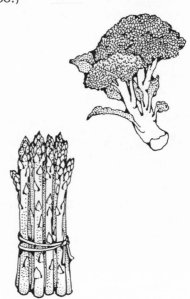

salad dressing
supreme

Now here's a dressing to end all dressing
(salads, I'm talking about!)

Ingredients:

1. *One cup saf-
flower oil (no
cholesterol).*
2. *3 tablespoon-
fuls wine vin-
egar or the juice
from 3 lemons*
3. *2 teaspoonfuls
Grey's Poupon
mustard*
4. *1 tablespoonful
olive oil
(splurge, buy
the virgin!)*
5. *Italian salad
dressing - dry
package.*

Mix all of above ingredients,
except the Italian salad dressing
dry mix. Store in refrigerator between uses - gets better with age (to
a point, don't we all!). Then, just
before use, sprinkle in a little bit
(less than 1 teaspoonful) of the dry
Italian salad mix - gives it zip!

. . .this, too was given me by
Dana Foster, that powerhouse
mighty mite. Great gal!

split pea soup

Another Paulette Vitrier Crabtree winner!

Ingredients:

1 (16 ounces) package of split green peas
1 medium size onion, peeled - get all the loose stuff off the outside and cut off both ends)
Ham Hocks (2 or 3, depending upon size)

Wash peas by running lots of water over them in some container with holes (strainer, colander, steamer, etc.). There are impurities in most packages and they need to be washed away. In an oven proof pot with a cover, add the above ingredients (just cut the onion into quarters) and enough water to almost cover the ham hocks.

Put into the oven, 250°, for 6 to 7 hours. Stir when you can, (don't stir if you can't!). If the soup is too "watery" for your taste, leave the cover off the pot for the last hour or two. This trick generally works for most everything. "Season to taste" just before serving, or just before re-heating. This is another favorite recipe that I usually make in large quantities and load up in my freezer by dividing into small containers.

baked beans, southern style

Another Crabtree Winner!

Ingredients:

1 (16 ounce) package of northern white beans

A few pieces of salt pork, cut up into 1" cubes (I trim a lot of the fat off)

1 big onion cut into quarters

1/4 cup dark brown sugar

1/2 teaspoonful mustard (I prefer dijon mustard and use almost 1 tablespoonful)

2 tablespoonfuls molasses (either the sulphured or unsulphured; I can't tell the difference!)

Wash the beans by rinsing in running water using any container with holes (strainer, colander, steamer, etc). Cover with water in a covered pot and let stand several hours (or even overnight is OK) until the beans have "popped".

Then, simply add all of the above ingredients to an oven proof covered pot and stick it in the oven, set at 250°, for 6 to 8 hours. Stir when you can, if you can! When finished, it may seem a bit watery to you, but it will thicken as it cools. Freezes well!

if you hate SPINACH, you'll LOVE this!

Ingredients:

2 handfuls of FRESH spinach (I mean SASSY fresh!)

2 tablespoonfuls margarine or butter

Salt & Pepper, to taste

Fresh ground nutmeg (for this recipe alone, I went out and bought a nut-meg mill and have never regretted it)

Have colander or large strainer and large spoon (preferably wooden) very handy - you will need these in a hurry!

Wash spinach thoroughly in cold water. Bring a large pot of water to a furious boil and dump in the spinach. IMMEDIATELY pour water and spinach into a colander or strainer, and turn off the stove. Put margarine, salt and pepper in pot (hot from the boiling water) and as soon as the margarine begins to melt, dump the spinach back in the pot. Stir with wooden spoon; add nutmeg (5 turns with the nutmeg mill), put in serving dish and FEAST. I often will make a meal of just this when I find really good spinach. The secret is that it is undercooked, plus the addition of nutmeg which most people don't recognize when giving you compliments on your gourmet super-abilities!

...This wonderful recipe given me by Bob Whittington, as close to me as the brother I never had. Bob is a true gourmet cook, world traveller, entrepreneur, world-class fisherman... I could go on, but you get the idea. (I hope you have at least one friend like Bob!)

wok cooking

Cooking "Stir Fry" is fun, quick, tasty and nutritious. You will spend more time preparing the food than cooking it - and you must be ready to sit right down and enjoy your meal AS SOON AS IT IS COOKED.

Invest in a good Wok - better to invest in a good Wok (heavy steel) than all of the paraphernalia associated with a Wok "set" - a stove top Wok is far superior to an electric one.

Here's a wonderful recipe to get the idea of this kind of cooking:

Ingredients:

- enough for 4 people, so adjust accordingly:
1 cup almonds
2 chicken breasts (double), cut into small pieces (1 1/2" cubes).
1 cup scallions, cut into 1 1/2 inch lengths (use both the white and green parts)
1 1/2 cups snow peas cut crosswise in half (roughly!)

Mix together the following five ingredients, and let them stand:
4 1/2 tablespoonfuls Sherry
4 1/2 tablespoonfuls Soy Sauce (low salt variety)
1 teaspoonful sugar
3 teaspoonfuls corn starch
1 garlic clove minced (optional). Can also use garlic powder.

Start the stove on high temperature and add 1 tablespoonful cooking oil (I prefer Safflower because it is cholesterol free). To the Wok, add the almonds and cook (constantly stirring) for about four or five minutes - until the nuts are golden brown (trust me, you'll know what I mean when you see it). After a couple of minutes, you will want to lower the cooking temperature setting a little. Remove the almonds and place in bowl until later.

(continued)

Without adding more oil, place all the chicken cubes in the Wok and cook until done -it will cook very quickly. (When stir frying, you cannot leave the stove - keep stirring -now you know the meaning of the expression "Stir Fry"!) When the chicken is nearing completion - it will be mostly white in color - cut a piece in two to see if the inside is mostly cooked. Add the snow peas, scallions and sherry-soy sauce mixture. Keep stirring for about 2 or 3 minutes. Finally, add the almonds, primarily to warm them up again. SERVE AND ENJOY!

A wonderful dish that goes with this is Basmati Rice (Indian). You can buy the rice at most health food stores. It takes less time to cook than domestic rice. Mix 1 cup of Basmati rice with 1 1/2 cups cold water (rinse rice first by running cold water on it while in a strainer). Bring to a boil, cover and let sit off the burner. It will be ready when the stir fry is!

Those are the basics - you can use pork or lamb in place of the chicken, wine rather than the sherry-soy sauce mixture, other vegetables or other kinds of nuts. Once you've used this recipe you'll be a better judge for your own tastes.

. . .this stir fry recipe (and Basmati rice) was cooked for me in my kitchen by a very dear lady whom I met on a trip to Costa Rica in 1988; Mrs. Lillian Talbot - a fascinating human being with the emphasis on human!

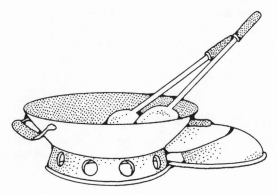

baked carrots

Clean, scrape and slice lengthwise in half one bunch of carrots. Wrap tightly as one bundle in aluminum foil. Bake in moderate (350°) oven for one hour - fabulous, retains the strong taste of the RAW carrot which is usually lost in cooked carrots. (Basically like baked potatoes).

. . .another Laurie Goring great contribution to this book!

(Author: Try in microwave with saran wrap - takes much less time and tastes just as good.)

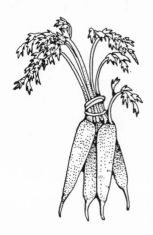

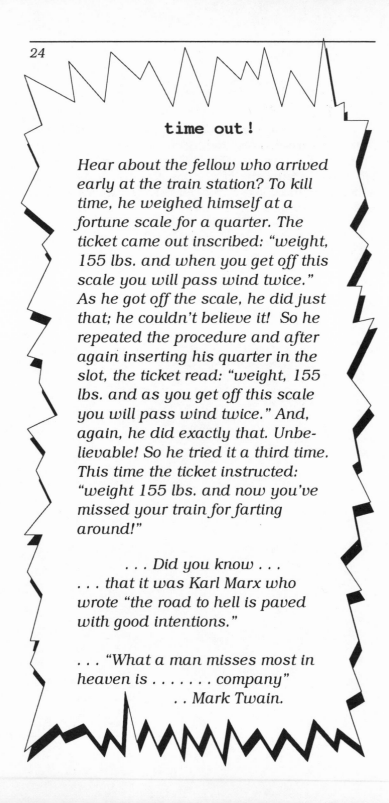

time out!

Hear about the fellow who arrived early at the train station? To kill time, he weighed himself at a fortune scale for a quarter. The ticket came out inscribed: "weight, 155 lbs. and when you get off this scale you will pass wind twice." As he got off the scale, he did just that; he couldn't believe it! So he repeated the procedure and after again inserting his quarter in the slot, the ticket read: "weight, 155 lbs. and as you get off this scale you will pass wind twice." And, again, he did exactly that. Unbelievable! So he tried it a third time. This time the ticket instructed: "weight 155 lbs. and now you've missed your train for farting around!"

. . . Did you know . . .
. . . that it was Karl Marx who wrote "the road to hell is paved with good intentions."

. . . "What a man misses most in heaven is . . . . company"
. . Mark Twain.

pecan cheese ball

Ingredients:

1 cup pecans
chopped fine
4 ounces low
cholesterol
cream cheese
2 tablespoonfuls
Roquefort
cheese
1 tablespoonful
non-cholesterol
margarine

With steel knife in your Cuisinart, (that is, if you were lucky enough to keep it, or perhaps you could only keep the blender, and if not that, either, use a plain old strong fork!) chop pecans. Add cream cheese, Roquefort, and margarine, mixing thoroughly. Shape with hands and place in dish - serve with variety of crackers (low cholesterol, of course!).

. . .a Madalyn Pollock recipe. She and her husband Sam, a fellow veterinarian, are the closest, dearest people and our friendship covers several decades! What a privilege to be their friend! I could write a book about their goodness!

pot roast delicioso

Ingredients:

1 Round (boned)
roast or pot
roast - any size,
but preferably
flat cut
1 package of
Lipton's dry
onion soup mix
1 can Campbell's
Cream of Mushroom soup

Use a large, double folded piece of aluminum foil placed in the bottom of an appropriately sized oven proof dish. Sprinkle the dry onion soup mix in the center of the foil and place the meat over the mix. Spoon out the mushroom soup (undiluted) on top of the meat. Fold the aluminum foil carefully and tightly around the meat. Crimp the aluminum foil with your fingers to seal. I

(continued)

have also used Reynolds Cooking Bags and they work well, too, particularly for larger pot roasts.

Place in oven set at 225° for 6 to 8 hours. This is another recipe which you can start before going to work in the morning and come home to a "beautifully delicious and nutritious" meal. When you open the foil up, put everything in the oven dish and serve. Makes its own gravy and the seasoning is just right. When cooking small pieces of pot roast, cut back on the amount of onion soup mix and mushroom soup. Enjoy!

. . . Given to me by Drenna Bishop, a Venice (Florida) veterinarian's wife who helped me conquer WordPerfect in a computer course at Venice High School.

. . a lesson in BREAST ANATOMY . .

It has been my experience that most women will tell you that a "chicken breast" consists of one-half of the breast meat on a normal chicken! And that most men, when queried, will tell you a chicken breast is made up of two halves. This can get complicated, as you can imagine, when passing chicken recipes around. So . . for the purposes of this book, a chicken breast is singular - one/half.

chicken divan extraordinare

Ingredients:

2 to 3 packages
frozen broccoli
6 to 8 chicken
breasts (halves)
1 cup mayonnaise
(cholesterol free)
1 can condensed
(Campbell's)
Cream of
Chicken soup
1/2 teaspoonful
curry powder -
gives a tangy
flavor
2 tablespoonfuls
lemon juice
(fresh juice is
best)
1/2 cup grated
cheddar or
parmesan
cheese
Bread crumbs
(Italian flavor
best, but any
will do)

Thaw and drain the broccoli. Place in bottom of oblong casserole (about 9x13 pyrex dish). Place the chicken breasts on top of the Broccoli. Mix the mayo, soup, curry powder and lemon juice and pour over the chicken. Sprinkle grated cheese and bread crumbs over everything. Place a dollop (1/2 teaspoonful) margarine (no cholesterol!) on top of each piece of chicken.

Bake 1 hour in oven at 350°. This meal will "hold in the oven (on low setting!) for 30 minutes or longer - in case your company is late! You can even cook this the day before needed and just warm up prior to serving.

. . .another recipe from that wonderful cook in Nokomis, Florida - Laurie Goring.

time out!

Did you hear about the teacher that called her quizzes "quizzicals?" . . wonder what she called her tests???

The only thing anger is good for is that it increases the arch in a cat's back!

Keep your eye on the doughnut . . . instead of the hole!

eggplant soup

This is more of an appetizer than a soup-meal.
Can be served hot or chilled.

Ingredients:

*1 medium size
eggplant, about
a pound
1 cup finely
chopped onion
2 tablespoonfuls
margarine (non
cholesterol)
2 large, ripe
tomatoes - about
1 1/4 pounds
1 cup finely
chopped green
pepper
1 cup yogurt,
optional
1 teaspoonful
minced garlic,
optional*

Preheat oven (that means turn it on NOW) to 500°. Place the eggplant on a doubled piece of aluminum foil, crimped up to catch any liquid, and bake for 40 minutes or longer. When ready, the eggplant should be totally soft throughout and collapsed. Remove the eggplant from the oven and let cool.

(If you still own a microwave oven, simply pierce eggplant 4 or 5 times with a thin sharp knife. Loosely wrap in paper toweling and place on a plate. Bake in microwave on high for 10 to 12 minutes or until really soft. Cool slightly, then scoop out pulp with a spoon.)

Heat the margarine in a saucepan and add onion and green pepper. Cook, stirring, until the liquid from the vegetables evaporates. I was surprised at how much liquid there is in onions and peppers!

Core the tomatoes and cut into one inch cubes (will amount to about 3 cups). Add this to the onion-pepper mixture and cook for about 30 minutes, stirring frequently.

(continued)

Spoon out the eggplant "meat" and cook with the onion-pepper-tomato mixture for about 5 minutes. Then blend the entire mixture in a blender or food processor until a puree'. Add the garlic and yogurt.

Serve hot or cold. I prefer to add a dollop of sour cream and fresh parsley to the top of the soup. Adding some lemon juice to the soup mixture enhances its flavor. This is a recipe you can fool around with and make it your very own specialty.

JOHNNY CARSON SAYS

"You can get more with a kind word and a gun than you can . . . with a kind word alone!"

a party dip that's a snap!

About 15 minutes before use, combine:

One package Lipton dry onion soup mix, with One container (about 2 cups) of Yogurt.

Stir well. That's it! Easy? Great with potato chips!

(Author: Even better if made several hours in advance or sits overnight in the refrigerator.)

. . . this recipe, and others to follow, given me by one of the ten foremost Canadian wildlife artists whom I was privileged to meet on a trip to the Yucatan: Brenda Carter.

oriental squash, delicio!

1 Winter squash (any variety, Brenda prefers Butternut)	Peel and cut to 1/2 golf ball size... (not necessarily round, unless you opt to be fancy ... a n d foot free?)
	Saute (fry) in margarine for 2 or 3 minutes, (teflon coated pan is best)
Then add: *Orange juice, to 1/4" depth of cooking pan.*	Cover and simmer for 5 minutes.
Then add: *2 pinches curry powder, and A small handful of raisins*	Re-cover and simmer another 10 minutes, adding water as necessary, (the orange juice evaporates). Just before serving, sprinkle with cashews.

This makes a hearty side dish when served with chicken or ham!

... this is another winner from that Canadian artist, Brenda Carter. Order her catalog by calling (613) 269-4433 - you'll be <u>very</u> glad you did!

"o" chicken shish-kabob

Ingredients:

10-15 cloves of garlic, minced
1/2 cup soy sauce
3/4 cup water
1/2 cup olive oil
1 tablespoonful powdered oregano
2-3 lbs. chicken breasts, cut in one inch squares

Combine all ingredients and marinate for at least 3 days in the refrigerator (or, if in a hurry, a few hours out on the counter). Add 1 onion and 1 green pepper (both cut up to about 1 1/2 inch size) to mixture and let stand, unrefrigerated, for 4 hours. Just prior to cooking, skewer the pepper and onion pieces next to the chicken (can also add chunks of pineapple on the skewer), and cook over charcoal.

. . . this recipe given me by a special guy, Rick Carter (brother of Brenda) whom I also met in the Yucatan. Rick lives in California and we can all sleep with less worry because he is a crew chief in the U.S. Air Force.

easy as pie
that's a pie!

Combine:

*1 stick margarine
(low cholesterol!)*
*Crumbled graham
crackers - use
about sixteen or
enough to give
the texture
necessary to
press into a pie
plate and form
the shape of a
crust.*

**Add to crust in
pie plate:**

*1 package dry
butterscotch
chips*
*1 package dry
chocolate chips*
*1 can <u>condensed
sweetened</u> milk
(not evaporated
milk!).*

Pour the milk over the chips. Do not mix. Bake at 325° for about one hour. Serve chilled, or cooled to room temperature - mmmm - good!

. . . this recipe given to me by a very neat gal whom I'm proud to say is my cousin. We met through one of the finest human beings ever, our Aunt Theresa (herself a noted dietician who could put together a wondrous meal with seemingly little effort), now deceased . . . and sorely missed. Oh! My cousin's name is . . Peggy Roy!

end of month meal

Here's one that makes stew meat taste like the finest steak!

Ingredients:

1 cup chopped
onions
2 lbs of cheap (but
fresh!) beef -
chuck with bone,
or stew beef,
etc.)
1 pint tomato juice

In an oven proof dish (pyrex is great!), place the onions under the beef and pour tomato juice over the meat. Cover and simmer for about 2 hours, until the meat is falling off the bone, or is tender when forked. Enjoy!

. . .this recipe given me by another cousin, Peggy Roy's sister, Juny Pick.

time out!

H.L. Mencken. . . . "When women kiss it always reminds me of prize fighters shaking hands."
(Author . .That's Bad!)

Aristotle. . . . "The vigorous are not better than the lazy during one-half of life, for all men are alike when asleep."

A NEW SLANT ON A BAKED POTATO

Cut a raw baking potato to about halfway through (lengthwise) and insert a bay leaf (or powdered bay) and cook in microwave (wrap in white paper napkin) for about 8 minutes. This gives the cooked potato a nutty flavor.

OR: Cook a baked potato in the usual way (oven or microwave), then slice in half, almost all the way through. Fill the slit with chopped broccoli, raw or cooked, or any vegetable to your liking. Then cover with Campbell's Cheddar Cheese soup and place back in oven to heat. This is really delicious. I've also tried it with cauliflower and carrots. This is one you can play around with and create your own recipe. Deliciosa!

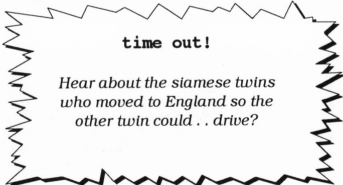

time out!

Hear about the siamese twins who moved to England so the other twin could . . drive?

marinara sauce
ala suglia

Ingredients:

1/4 cup olive oil - buy the best. "I like Berio or Bertolli as well as any" says the author of this recipe.

6 cloves of garlic, minced

1 can (28 ounces) Italian whole tomatoes

Fresh basil, 3 stalks - and a pinch of Oregano

Heat olive oil in frying pan and cook minced garlic until slightly golden. Drain tomatoes in a colander, saving the drippings in a bowl. Then chop up the tomatoes, again draining the drippings into the bowl via a colander. (The reason for this: you want to get as much water out of the tomatoes as possible, so that they are fried in the olive oil rather than boiled.) Add the "dry" tomatoes to the frying pan and toss constantly for about 2 minutes. Add 3 stalks of fresh basil and a pinch of oregano. Add the tomato drippings and continue to cook for about 2 minutes. Salt and pepper to taste. Mix with freshly cooked pasta and some fresh ground parmesan cheese to taste. <u>Fit for a King</u>!

. . . this recipe given me by a very special human being - truly, one of the most special that I know! Nick Suglia and his lovely wife, Ann. Marinara is Italian for Mariner (sailor) and it was Nick who was to be our cook on our sailboat, Marshbound, during an ill-fated voyage to Bermuda in 1972 (remember Hurricane Agnes? - we'll never forget!). But that's another book . . in the making!

time out!

Frank Sinatra agrees with me, so does Dean Martin, Anne Bancroft, Luciano Pavarotti, Charles Nelson Reilly, Vic Damone, Carl Reiner and Mel Brooks - if we were on a desert island with only one food to live on, what one food would we all choose?? "PASTA!"

MEET MY NEW FRIEND "SUZI"

Suzi - a garlic press made by Zeiss (Switzerland) - the best garlic press I've ever seen. It has very close tolerance and is easy to clean because it comes with a plastic comb device which easily clean the holes in the press. Available at Williams/Sonoma mail order.

Lifetime investment for about $13.00.

spaghetti sauce "by the two's"

Ingredients:

- 2 quart jars of Prego (or your favorite!) spaghetti sauce
- 2 lbs. of lean ground turkey or extra lean ground beef
- 2 medium onions
- 2 medium green peppers
- 2 large bay leaves
- 2 teaspoonfuls oregano
- 2 tablespoonfuls soy sauce
- 2 tablespoonfuls sugar
- 2 small cans of black sliced olives
- 2x2x2 cloves of garlic, minced (ED: this = 8!)
- 8 ounces fresh mushrooms, sliced lengthwise in thirds
- 1 bottle of beer
- 1/2 cup sherry or red wine (sherry is better!)

In a large pot empty the two jars of sauce and simmer on medium heat. Add black pepper to taste, sugar, green peppers, oregano, bay leaves, beer and soy sauce. Stir occasionally when it starts to boil.

Meanwhile, in a large frying pan, cook the meat over high heat. As soon as it is no longer pink, drain into a container in which you can remove the fat and add the juice to the sauce. Place the meat back in the pan and continue cooking until it is thoroughly browned (this should take at least another 20 minutes). Add meat to the sauce.

Reheat the frying pan and then cover the bottom of the pan with olive oil. Add the onions and cook until brown and then add these onions to the sauce. Deglaze the pan by pouring 1/2 of the wine in the pan and heat. Pour the rest of the wine in the sauce.

Again reheat the frying pan, add margarine and saute the mushrooms together with the garlic (and deglazing wine). Pour off some of the fluids and continue to cook until the mushrooms have browned. Add to the sauce.

(continued)

Cover the sauce pot and continue to cook at low heat for at least 4 hours. The sauce should bubble every few seconds, but remember that the temperature will go up when you cover the pot, so be sure and check it a few minutes after you put the lid on - watch that you don't burn the sauce on the bottom.

At the end of the 4th hour, remove the lid and continue to cook (reduces the fluid by evaporation) until you can place a spoonful of the sauce on a tipped plate and it doesn't run!

Bon Appetit! *(Author: HINT: a tossed salad, some garlic bread and a glass or two of Chianti adds up to pure perfection!)*

one dish colorful pasta delight

Serves four as a side dish - or two (hungry!) as a main course.

Ingredients:

8 ounce package
of fresh tricolor
pasta shells
8 ounce can
artichoke hearts
1 tomato, fresh,
(fist size)
handful of spin-
ach leaves
5 sprigs of
cilantro (some-
times called
fresh coriander)
1 teaspoonful
garlic (use the
pre-chopped, in
the jar), or 3
cloves, minced.
1 tablespoonful
olive oil
Black pepper to
taste.

Cook the pasta according to package directions.

Meanwhile, drain the artichoke hearts and chop. Slice the tomato and chop. Remove the thick stems from the spinach and tear into small pieces. Chop the cilantro.

Drain the pasta, and put the pan back on low heat. Add the oil and garlic. Toss in the rest of the ingredients; add the pasta. Cover and turn off the heat. After 5 minutes, toss and serve.

All of these ingredients can be picked up at the store on the way home; this dish takes about 15 minutes preparation time.

...this is an extraordinary recipe given me by an extraordinary lady, Kate Black, an accomplished sailor of Virgin Islands fame and the daughter of my friend and cardiologist, also an avid sailor! Kate also keeps her Dad's office in tow!

time out!

. . . .don't regret growing old - it's a privilege denied to some!

If sex is such a natural phenom-enon, how come there are so many books on how to?
. . . . .Bette Midler

For the sin they do by two and two they must pay for one by one
. . . Rudyard Kipling

To abstain from sin when one can no longer sin is to be forsaken by sin, not to forsake it!
. . . .St. Augustine

From Oscar Wilde . . . "There is no sin except stupidity!"

fettucini

For the stomach, not the heart!

Combine and heat:
1/2 pint light cream
1 stick butter melted
1 cup parmesan cheese

Pour over cooked (al dente) pasta! Al dente means that you cook the pasta only until it is just tender but still resistant to your bite.

That's it! Nothing to it - and it's great! Enough "sauce" for 8 ounces of fettucini pasta or vermicelli, pre-cooked! Serves two - worth a tossed salad, garlic bread and . . . chianti wine. Add some candles, slow music and . . . who knows!

a jogger's...
(harvard) hamburger

. . . from a special Harvard man, Larry Spang; special, because he's married to my daughter, Susan, who says, "Whenever Larry needs to be a "bachelor" for an evening, he uses this special recipe:"

Light the grill
Go for a jog
Come back; shower
Put thick hamburger patty on the grill
Toast bun or English Muffin
Add favorite toppings

. . . Susan hastens to add that Larry is rarely a "bachelor!"

london broil

(end of month!)

Use flank steak or other less expensive cuts of beef and marinate at room temperature for about 4 hours in Italian Wishbone salad dressing; pierce meat with a fork. Meat will turn a grayish color. Or, if more convenient, marinate overnight in refrigerator (cover dish with lid or saran wrap/aluminum foil).

Broil on grill or bake in oven at 350°. Time will depend upon weight and thickness of meat.

. . . given to me by a sometime dancing partner, Marian Male!

my susan's simple swift savory supper

A simple dinner which has infinite variations:

In a casserole or baking dish, place either (or a combo):

Shrimps, scallops or whitefish
Top with your favorite Salsa Sauce and shredded Cheddar Cheese

Bake at 350° until it looks done, (flakes with a fork and cheese has melted) . . about 10 minutes or so.

. . . I'm glad, in a way, that I have only one daughter, because I can happily announce publicly that Susan is my favorite daughter! (I can't conceive that she wouldn't be anyway!) Most decidedly, when daughters and sisters were handed out in Heaven, I was luckily first in line! (Most definitely, SONS, TOO! - I'm blessed with two great ones!!)

susie's cheesecake

Ingredients:

Crust:
1 package gra-
   ham crackers,
   crushed
1/2 cup melted
   butter
2 teaspoonfuls
   cinnamon
2 tablespoonfuls
   sugar
1 cup chopped
   walnuts

Blend above ingredients and press into a 9 inch buttered spring form pan.

Cheesecake:
24 oz cream
   cheese - low fat
1 cup sugar
1 teaspoonful
   vanilla
3 eggs
1 1/2 pints sour
   cream - low fat

Cream (that means to combine until smooth) the cream cheese and sugar. Add vanilla and eggs. Mix well. Add sour cream and blend all together. Pour into spring form pan and bake at 350° for 40 to 55 minutes. Leave in the oven for one hour (with oven turned off and the oven door cracked open).

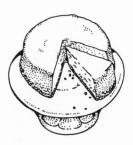

. . . this recipe is from Susan Lewis, an interesting lady who years ago ran a wonderful intimate restaurant, "Cafe In The Mews," on Siesta Key, Sarasota, Florida. I met Susan through my own Susan (daughter!) who at one time worked there.

tasty
eggplant parmesan

Here's a great microwave recipe:

Ingredients:

1 medium egg-
  plant
1 slice of white
  bread, crumbled
1/4 cup grated
  Parmesan
  cheese
2 tablespoonfuls
  butter, melted
2 cups spaghetti
  sauce
1 1/2 to 2 cups
  shredded
  Mozzarella
  cheese

1. Pierce the skin of the egg-plant several times; arrange egg-plant on a paper towel in a shallow glass oven-proof dish. Heat 4 1/2 to 5 1/2 minutes on high until the eggplant is almost tender. Let cool, then peel if desired, and slice into 1/2 inch pieces.

2. Meanwhile, combine bread crumbs, parmesan cheese and but-ter. In 1 1/2 quart casserole dish alternately layer the spaghetti sauce, eggplant, crumb mixture and Mozzarella cheese. Microwave on high for 10 1/2 to 11 1/2 minutes until heated through. To heat by temperature, insert probe into cen-ter of casserole and set tempera-ture-cook at 160°.

3. Let stand, covered for 5 min-utes before serving.

4. Variations: Saute mush-rooms and onions and mix with spaghetti sauce. And/or: dice black or Greek olives and sprinkle on top of the layer of Mozzarella cheese. Some like to season this dish with garlic - optional.

(continued)

   . . . sounds good, doesn't it! IT IS! The man who gave me this recipe, Rick Frankford, has a lovely wife, Diana, who significantly helps with the development of our BioPark at Sarasota.

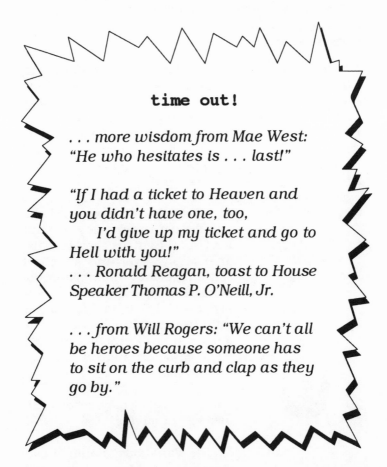

time out!

. . . more wisdom from Mae West: "He who hesitates is . . . last!"

"If I had a ticket to Heaven and you didn't have one, too,
   I'd give up my ticket and go to Hell with you!"
. . . Ronald Reagan, toast to House Speaker Thomas P. O'Neill, Jr.

. . . from Will Rogers: "We can't all be heroes because someone has to sit on the curb and clap as they go by."

orange cinnamon french toast— ala cafe in the mews

Ingredients:

Bread
3 eggs
3/4 cup milk
*1 tablespoonful orange rind**
1 teaspoonful cinnamon
*2 teaspoonfuls orange extract**
1 cup orange juice (optional)

Mix all ingredients together in an electric blender and blend at highest speed. Pour into a bowl with enough room to hold the bread. Cut the bread in half so you have two triangles. Quickly dip into the batter - do not soak the bread. Place in a hot skillet with melted butter (preferably unsalted). Fry on both sides until nicely browned. Serve with syrup or powdered sugar! Any left over? Freeze, then reheat in microwave oven. Serves four to six.

This is also nice to do with french bread—sliced at the same thickness or slightly thicker.

* "About the rind," Susan says, "I really only use rind from tangerines or tangelo oranges. When they aren't in season, I use McCormick's orange rind. Also use McCormick's orange extract."

. . .another winner from Cafe In The Mews chef/owner, Susan Lewis.

meatballs
...by joyce!

Ingredients:

1 lb lean ground
beef, or veal, or
turkey
1 / 2 cup corn
flakes,
crumbled
1 / 2 cup evapo-
rated milk
1 / 4 cup finely
chopped onion
1 / 4 cup chili
sauce
1 tablespoonful
Worcestershire
sauce
1 teaspoonful salt
1 teaspoonful
pepper

Blend meat with corn flake crumbs and milk. Add remaining ingredients and blend lightly. With wet hands, shape into small balls (recipe will yield about 36 which will give you some idea of ball size - smaller than a golf ball, larger than a grape!). Place on cookie sheet and bake in 400 degree oven for 12 to 15 minutes.

sauce
...by joyce!

Ingredients:

8 ounce can
    tomato sauce
1/2 cup ketchup
2 tablespoon-
    fuls brown
    sugar
2 tablespoonfuls
    finely chopped
    onion
2 tablespoonfuls
    pickle relish,
    drained
2 tablespoonfuls
    water
2 tablespoonfuls
    Worcestershire
    sauce
1 tablespoonful
    vinegar
Dash of pepper

Combine tomato sauce, ketchup, sugar and onion. Cook over medium heat until sugar is dissolved and onion is tender. Stir in remaining ingredients and heat to steaming. Pour over meat balls. Bon Appetite!

. . . these recipes given me by Joyce Battaglia . . . interesting gal, and a fine cook!

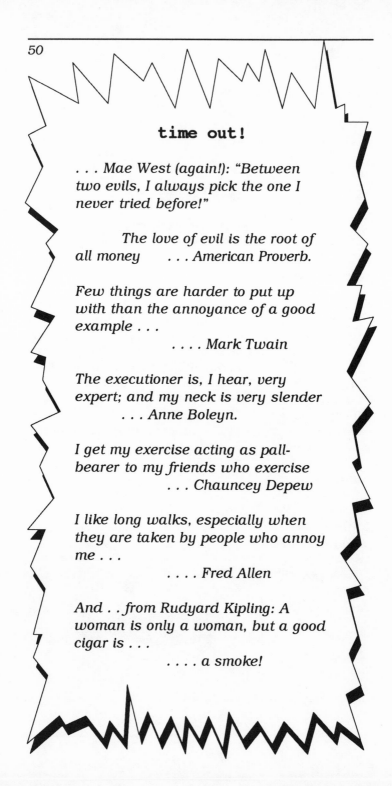

time out!

. . . Mae West (again!): "Between two evils, I always pick the one I never tried before!"

The love of evil is the root of all money   . . . American Proverb.

Few things are harder to put up with than the annoyance of a good example . . .
.... Mark Twain

The executioner is, I hear, very expert; and my neck is very slender . . . Anne Boleyn.

I get my exercise acting as pall-bearer to my friends who exercise . . . Chauncey Depew

I like long walks, especially when they are taken by people who annoy me . . .
.... Fred Allen

And . . from Rudyard Kipling: A woman is only a woman, but a good cigar is . . .
.... a smoke!

kitchen equipment

A word or two about **kitchen equipment**. Buy the best equipment your budget allows rather than cheap items you will only have to replace later on, which will only prove to be false economy!

My idea of a **beginner bachelor-cook kitchen**:

- array of good stainless pots (I bought Revere and have never regretted it), probably 4 or 5 different sizes (I find that I use the 1/2, 1 and 2 quart sizes most often.)
- one medium size frying pan - preferably one that matches a pot so that you can use the same lid.
- Wok, if you like Oriental. Buy a good one, not electric!
- set of good kitchen knives and a steel for sharpening them. (If you don't know how to use a sharpening steel, ask any butcher - they'll be delighted for your interest!)
- vegetable steamer basket, stainless and collapsible so that it will fit inside most size pots.
- coffee maker, if you like coffee. Otherwise, a jar of instant coffee will do nicely!
- tea pot
- set of mixing bowls
- rubber spatula
- wooden mixing spoon
- set of measuring spoons
- 2 cup capacity measuring cup
- pot holders. Actually long mitts are better - they protect your wrists!
- pyrex dishes:
    - 8 x 8 x 2"
    - 8 x 11 1/2 x 2"
    - 1 quart casserole dish with cover
- vegetable peeler
- metal spatula or pancake turner
- soup ladle
- tea strainer (unless you always use tea bags - *ugh! Author*)

(continued)

GARAGE/ESTATE SALES can be a bachelor's best friend when equipping his kitchen. But don't overbuy, and <u>don't buy junk!</u>

Cleaning Copper Bottoms! Save your old citrus - orange, grapefruit, lime, it doesn't matter! Cut in half, pour salt on the open citrus and rub on copper squeezing the citrus juice onto the copper as needed. May need a little elbow grease. Add more salt as needed. You'll be surprised how this cleans copper - any copper!

Disposables:

♦ array of plastic, self-sealing bags - good for leftovers in the refrigerator or freezer. Can easily identify the contents. Squeeze out as much air as possible before sealing.

♦ Saran Wrap. I think it's better than any other brand. BUT . . practice. The first time you use it, you'll swear you need 2 men and a boy to keep it from sticking to itself. Figure the first time, you'll end up pounding it into a ball and throwing it against the kitchen wall. OK. Next time, get one side adhered to the container you're covering. Cheer up! You'll get the hang of it! The reason why I like Saran Wrap is that it is easier to work with than all the other brands I've tried . . believe it or not!

♦ aluminum foil (buy the best, it's stronger!).

♦ waxed paper. If you have a microwave, waxed paper is ideal for covering food while it is cooking.

For the more ambitious, experienced bachelor-cook:

♦ electric egg beater
♦ electric blender (Osterizer) - variable speed
♦ kitchen radio! Nice to hear music while you're cooking
♦ Cuisinart (food processor)
♦ 8 quart stainless pot with cover
♦ 9 inch spring-form pan
♦ pyrex pie pan
♦ 12 inch bundt cake pan
♦ stainless steel cookie sheet
♦ cake rack (for cooling)

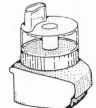

time out!

The best executive is the one who has sense enough to pick good men to do what he wants done, and self-restraint enough to keep from meddling with them while they do it.
Theodore Roosevelt

In statesmanship get the formalities right, never mind about the moralities.
Mark Twain

A statesman is a politician who's been dead ten or fifteen years.
Harry S. Truman

ratatouille vitrier

Here's a real winner from that divine cook, Paulette Vitrier Crabtree:

Ingredients:

1 medium egg-plant, partially peeled (about 1/2 surface peeled) and cubed to 1" size

1 small bunch of parsley, chopped

1 green pepper, cut into 1" strips, seeds and membrane removed

1 red pepper, cut into 1" strips, seeds and membrane removed

1 large zucchini, cubed

1 small box of sliced mush-rooms, or 7 large, sliced

1 teaspoonful fresh garlic, or 3 cloves, minced

1 Bermuda onion, cut to 1" cubes

5 tablespoonfuls olive oil

If you're having a dinner party, prepare as above and arrange all ingredients on a cookie tray or other display. (Remember that eggplant turns brown rather quickly when left in the air, so prepare eggplant just before your guests arrive!)

The principle in cooking Ratatouille is to use high heat, frequent stirring and then simmer on low heat. So, cover bottom of saucepan (best is a good skillet with a cover; I don't have a large enough one, so I use my largest saucepan) with 5 tablespoonfuls or so of olive oil, and set on high heat. Cook the minced garlic then add peppers, onion, zucchini, eggplant and mushrooms stirring constantly, but gently, caring not to mash the contents. Add more olive oil as needed. Add salt and pepper, oregano, and tomatoes (not the juice - save for other recipes such as Marinara Sauce ala Suglia!). You will begin to notice that there is an accumulation of vegetable juices in the bottom of the pan. When this occurs, reduce heat from high to simmer and cover, stirring occasionally, for 30 - 35 minutes, or until the onions are thoroughly cooked.

2 dog food size
  cans whole
  tomatoes,
  quartered and
  drained, but
  save the juice
1 tablespoonful
  oregano
2 teaspoonfuls
  table salt.
  Eggplant needs
  a lot of salt
  because it has a
  bland taste.
1/8 lb. shaved
  ham, per per-
  son. Get this in
  the Deli section
  of your food
  market. (Baked
  is tastier than
  boiled!)
2 slices of Mozza-
  rella cheese per
  serving

In individual bowls, line the bottom with shaved ham (ask the butcher to shave it for you - you can use either boiled or baked ham: boiled is less expensive, baked has more flavor. Use 1/8 lb per portion), spoon the Ratatouille over the ham and cover with slices of mozzarella cheese. "Tent" each bowl with aluminum foil (tenting: leave air space between the top of the ingredients and the aluminum foil - I like to think of an imaginary tennis ball sitting on top of the food, and "tent" over it!). Bake for 10 minutes or so at 325° - until the cheese is nicely melted.

Serve with warm French bread and a fresh salad. A meal fit for a king!

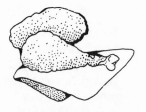

a "hull"
of a chicken!

This recipe will quickly become a favorite of your epicurean escapades:

Ingredients:

*5 or 6 chicken
pieces*
*Equal parts of
flour (wheat is
best, and more
nutritious) and
corn flakes,
crumbled*
*1 egg - may need
to add a little
water or milk to
stretch the liquid
for dipping*

Dip chicken parts in beaten egg and coat with flour/corn flake mixture by shaking both in a plastic bag. Place in pyrex baking dish, skin side up, and bake at 325° for about an hour or until no pink meat remains. It is not necessary to pre-grease the baking dish.

. . . This great recipe was given to me by Mary Mason Hull, a very special lady whom I haven't known very long, . . . but whom I have known a lifetime! I hope you will soon meet your special lady and enjoy life once again!

tomato soup
ala ambrosia

Here's a recipe that Mary Mason Hull devised while we were enjoying delicious "home-made" tomato soup at the Ambrosia Restaurant, San Jose, Costa Rica!

Make the Marinara Sauce, ala Suglia, found on page 36, with the following deviations:

Add an onion or two, cut up, and saute with the garlic - use about twice the amount of garlic as called for in the Marinara recipe.

Use the canned, peeled tomatoes as per the Marinara recipe, but add equal amounts of fresh tomatoes, peeled*, cut up and drained just like the canned tomatoes. (Use very ripe fresh tomatoes).
(* see #1, "Tip" of the Hull, found on page 58)

Fry all of the tomatoes together, adding much more oregano (three times as much!) and a dash of nutmeg. If you have it, add a bay leaf or two (remove prior to serving!). Add all of the tomato juice plus a small amount of water or canned tomato juice if needed (it usually is - depends on the juiciness of your fresh tomatoes). Put everything together in a covered pot and let simmer for a few minutes. Add 1 teaspoonful of sugar, or to your taste.

Serve with fresh hot bread or rolls and DON'T FORGET to add a dollop of light sour cream to each bowl served! This recipe is fit for a king! P.S. I had not one, but two bowls of this delicious nectar from the garden that day at Ambrosia!
(Author: This version is every bit as good!)

from the "tip" of the hull

That's right. Kitchen tips from my best friend, Mary Mason Hull - herself a home economics teacher!

1. To peel a fresh tomato, stick it on a fork and dip into boiling water for about 30 seconds; the skin will peel right off! Do the same with a clove of garlic after snipping off the ends. (This important tidbit given me by my BioPark cohort, Jan Miller!)

2. If you over salt almost any food, add a raw, peeled and diced potato while cooking the over salted food and the potato will absorb the salt; throw the potato pieces away!

3. Because of their acidity, tomatoes are usually improved if a little sugar is added while cooking. Try it to your own taste.

4. When using a pyrex (glass) dish for baking, lower the oven temperature by 25°!

5. When a recipe calls for "flour," use all-purpose, enriched flour unless the type of flour is specified. This is true of most cookbooks.

a word about eggs: chicken, that is!

"A hen is only an egg's way of making another egg." . . . Samuel Butler

Recently, I found in my food market a new kind of egg - a low cholesterol egg, claiming to have no more than 185 mg of cholesterol per egg. From the label: "Chickens respond to dietary changes in much the same way we humans do. These eggs were produced by hens that are fed a wholesome, all-natural diet containing four grains: corn, wheat, oats and rice. This nutritious diet is high in protein and fiber, yet low in fat - the same type of diet many doctors recommend to their health conscious patients. This healthy diet, along with carefully controlled temperature, lighting and other environmental factors, allow our hens to produce these eggs with an average cholesterol content of 185 mg. per large egg." Brand name is *4-Grain* eggs. They are a bit more expensive, about $.30 extra per dozen. Now you know!

garlic sticks

Pre-heat oven to 350°. Brush melted margarine on slices of enriched white bread and sprinkle with garlic salt. (*Author: garlic powder just as good!*) Cut into strips and place on an ungreased cookie sheet (or aluminum foil) and bake until golden brown - about 12 to 15 minutes. Enjoy!

time out!

NEVER believe in NEVER!

C-A-N-'T . . . just another awful four-letter word!

Let Your Dreams, Not Your Regrets, Take Command of your Life! What Dream Would <u>You</u> Dream, if you <u>knew</u> you could succeed! You Can Go Anywhere From Where You Are!
. . . . Your Future Is Your Friend!

Someday is . . . TODAY!!

Failure just means that you have not yet succeeded! Never allow a fractured experience to shape your future!

When you feel at your lowest, remember this: There Is Nowhere To Go . . . BUT UP!! Problems are Guidelines, NOT Stop Signs!

gabriella's
great chicken
delight

Here's a recipe guaranteed to not only please the palate, but your guests will beg for the recipe! Direct from Costa Rica!

Use cut-up pieces of chicken, skinned, and arrange in a pyrex baking dish; the quantity depends upon the size of your party!

Add enough lemon juice to cover the pieces of chicken, add salt to taste and at least one whole head, or bulb (that's a clump of cloves!) of garlic, peeled and minced. This sounds like an awful lot of garlic, but trust me, it's not. Cover with saran wrap and place in refrigerator overnight. This is called "marinating"; the lemon juice et al is called the marinade. Next day, roll the wet pieces of chicken in flour and fry in olive oil!

. . . This recipe given to me by a delightful artist-hotelier from Costa Rica, Gabriella Zeledon. She owns and operates the "Llamo del Bosque" - a delightful bed/breakfast Inn in Curridabat (an eastern suburb of San Jose, Costa Rica), which I would highly recommend! Direct dial from Anywhere USA for reservations: 011-506-24-62-58; you'll be glad you did!

salad
...by mary

Here's an interesting twist on a salad for a party!

Ingredients:

4 cups raw
  Broccoli, cut up
  into bite-size
  pieces
1/2 cup chopped
  celery
1/4 cup chopped
  onion
1/2 cup raisins

Sprinkle with bacon bits after adding salad dressing.

Dressing:
1 cup mayonnaise
  (non choles-
  terol!)
1/2 cup sugar
1/4 cup vinegar

Blend together:

straight from heaven hawiian cake

Ingredients:

2 cups flour
2 cups sugar
2 eggs, beaten
2 teaspoonfuls
   baking soda
1 can (20 oz)
   crushed pine-
   apple in juice,
   not syrup
   (available
   both ways -
   check the label)
1 cup chopped
   nuts (macad-
   amia nuts are
   best)
1 teaspoonful
   vanilla extract
1 cup dried,
   flaked coconut

Mix all together in a 9" x 12" baking pan. Bake at 350° for 30 to 35 minutes. Cool and frost.

Frosting:

3/4 cup powdered
   (xxxxx) sugar
1/2 stick marga-
   rine (no choles-
   terol!)
4 oz cream cheese
   (low fat!)

Mix together and frost! (Author: this will become one of your favorite easy desserts!)

mashed potatoes

Cook some new (red or boiling type) potatoes and then add non-fat yogurt, pepper and a tiny touch of Dijon mustard. Mash or whip with beaters.

Simple, good and great tasting!

peanut brittle

Here's an easy one if you have an electric fry pan. Otherwise it might be disastrous!

Heat electric fry pan to 400° then add 3 cups sugar and stir until melted. (If you don't have an electric fry pan that can be set at 400°, you might TRY using a regular pot and a cooking thermometer. Important NOT to overheat and burn, which is very easy to do!) Stir frequently with a wooden spoon (metal spoon will get too hot and burn the sugar).

Stir into the melted sugar 1 cup salted peanuts.

Pour into a greased tray (with sides) to desired thickness. When cool, break apart. Delicious!

walnut chopped "liver" —by kay

Ingredients:

2 onions, medium size, chopped coarsely
2 hard cooked eggs (or whites of 3 eggs, hard cooked)
1 SMALL can of peas, drained (or 1 small can of string beans)
12 walnuts
1 tablespoonful canola oil.

Saute (fry) the onions in the oil until golden brown. Let cool slightly. Put onions and the remaining ingredients into your electric blender (or cuisinart, if you're still lucky enough to have it!) and mix until well blended and looks like pate'. Add salt and black pepper to taste! Serve with cocktail rye bread or whole wheat crackers or whatever you have on hand. NO ONE will be able to guess the ingredients. Looks and tastes like fine pate'!

. . . Another clever idea from the kitchen of Kay Elman!

time out!

"Laziness travels so slowly that poverty soon overtakes him.". . . Benjamin Franklin

Aim at nothing, and you WILL succeed!!

Talent is spelled W - O - R - K.

It's better to do <u>something</u> <u>imperfectly</u> than to do <u>nothing</u> perfectly!

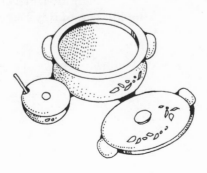

super-easy coconut pie ala elman!

Here's a super recipe given me by a super lady, Kay Elman, a cherished friend for many years (Ben, her husband, too!).

Mix together in medium mixing bowl:

2 eggs, slightly beaten
1 cup sugar
1 cup low fat milk, added gradually
1/4 cup flour
1/2 teaspoonful baking powder
1 teaspoonful vanilla
1/2 stick melted margarine
1 can (8 ounce) flaked coconut

Blend all together and pour into lightly greased pie pan. Bake at 350° for 30 minutes or until lightly browned. Makes its own crust! Serve when cooled (*author: if you can wait!*).

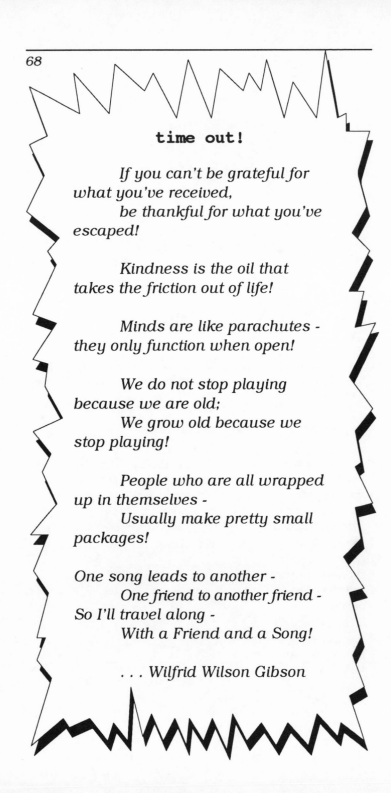

time out!

If you can't be grateful for
what you've received,
be thankful for what you've
escaped!

Kindness is the oil that
takes the friction out of life!

Minds are like parachutes -
they only function when open!

We do not stop playing
because we are old;
We grow old because we
stop playing!

People who are all wrapped
up in themselves -
Usually make pretty small
packages!

One song leads to another -
One friend to another friend -
So I'll travel along -
With a Friend and a Song!

. . . Wilfrid Wilson Gibson

wackie cake, by mary!

Sift together into an 8" x 8" baking pan:

*1 1/2 cups all
  purpose flour*
*3 tablespoonfuls
  cocoa powder*
*1 teaspoonful
  baking soda*
1 cup sugar
*1/2 teaspoonful
  salt*

Mix together:
*5 tablespoonfuls
  melted butter
  (follow grada-
  tions on wrap-
  per to measure)*
1 cup warm water
*1 teaspoonful
  vinegar*
*1 teaspoonful
  vanilla*

Pour this liquid into the flour mixture, mix thoroughly with a fork. Bake at 350° for 25 to 30 minutes.

Frost with broiled frosting.

Frosting:
*1/4 cup soft
  butter or marga-
  rine (1/2 stick)*
*3 tablespoonfuls
  cream (Rich's
  CoffeeRich non-
  dairy creamer
  OK)*
*1/3 cup chopped
  nuts*
*3/4 cup grated
  coconut*

Mix ingredients, spread on warm cake, set oven dial to "broil," and place about 3" under the broiler (the heating element above the food) until the frosting browns (about 5 to 8 minutes)!

bulgarian eggpant dip -for eggplant haters!!

Roast a PIERCED whole eggplant in microwave for about 10 minutes or until really nice and soft! Let cool. Remove flesh of eggplant and place in food processor (or blender) and pulse (short jerks of power). Add 1 small can of drained jalapeno peppers, 1 or 2 cut up firm tomatoes (1 if large, 2 if small), 3 or 4 cloves of garlic, salt to taste (1 teaspoonful or thereabouts) and pulse. When blended, add 1 or 2 tablespoonfuls of oil and pulse. Flavors improve overnight (store in refrigerator). No one will guess the ingredients!

. . . Another culinary delight with lovely Kay Elman's name on it!

pasta with garlic

Ingredients:

*8 ounces spa-
ghetti (thin, fat
or whatever)*
*8 garlic cloves,
chopped coarse*
*1/3 cup (extra
virgin!) olive oil*
*1/3 cup minced
fresh flat leaf
parsley*
*1/4 teaspoonful
dried hot pepper
flakes*
*8 tablespoonfuls
(1/2 cup) liquid
from the cooked
spaghetti*
Salt and black pep-
per to taste

Cook spaghetti in boiling water for 7 to 9 minutes. DRAIN...but reserve 1/2 cup of cooking liquid. Use same heavy pot and cook garlic cloves in the oil over moderate heat until golden. Add the parsley and red pepper flakes. Cook for 30 seconds or so. Add the drained spaghetti and pour the 1/2 cup of reserved cooking liquid. Add salt and black pepper to taste. Toss until fairly well mixed. Should serve FOUR especially if you serve with crisp garlic bread and a nice bowl of salad with garlic dressing. Add some red wine and it's a meal for guests (*author: fit for a king!*).

. . . Here's another recipe from that very special human being, Kay Elman!

garbanzo bean dip —from the elman kitchen

"Gotta do this a bit in advance...cuz it tastes better if kept overnight in the frig. Dump 1 can of garbanzo beans (liquid and all!) into blender or processor; blend. Add 2 tablespoonfuls of tahini (buy at health store), 2 cloves of garlic and a dash of tamari sauce (at health food store) OR use soy sauce. Blend. Taste it. If it doesn't grab you, adjust flavor by adding beans, tahini, garlic or soy sauce. After you have perfected YOUR recipe, you can double or triple it for a party! Serve with pita bread cut in eighths surrounding the bean dip. Sliced red onion rings circling the dip add color and flavor. NO ONE WILL GUESS THESE INGREDIENTS!"

joni's beer bread

. . . I don't know who Joni is, but this quick, GREAT bread comes from the oven of Kay Elman, a wonderful human being!

"Mix together 3 CUPS SELF-RISING FLOUR, 3 TABLESPOONFULS SUGAR and 1 CAN ROOM TEMPERATURE REGULAR BEER. Slop into a greased loaf pan and bake in 350° oven for one hour. The aroma will knock your socks off...but wait until the bread has sufficiently cooled before you attack it! Great the next day (IF you can wait that long) toasted for breakfast."

health
—from kay elman
12 bean soup

Ingredients:

2 cups or so of 12
   bean mixture
   (available at
   health food
   stores and
   cheaper there,
   too) 2 quarts
   water
1 lb. or so of thick,
   diced ham (or 1
   or 2 ham hocks -
   ham is less
   caloric)
1 large onion,
   chopped
1 or 2 chopped
   carrots
1 or 2 cloves
   garlic, minced
1/2 to 3/4 tea-
   spoonful salt

Add:
   1 can (16 ounce)
   chopped toma-
   toes with the
   liquid, and
1/2 small can of
   CHOPPED green
   chilis (hot Mexi-
   can peppers).

Wash the beans well. Put in heavy pot or Dutch oven and cover with water to 2 inches above beans. Let soak overnight. In morning, drain beans. Then add next 6 ingredients (water, ham, vegetables and seasoning).

Cover and bring to a boil. Reduce heat and simmer 1 1/2 hours or until beans are tender.

Simmer 30 minutes. Serve with pumpernickel rolls for maximum nourishment. Enjoy!

super kay's super scotch scones

Ingredients:

2 cups flour
2 tablespoonfuls
  sugar
2 teaspoonfuls
  baking powder
1/2 teaspoonful
  baking soda
1/2 cup cold
  margarine, or
  butter, cut into
  chunks
1 cup chopped
  walnuts
1/2 cup raisins
3/4 cup butter-
  milk *

In large bowl, combine flour, sugar, baking powder and baking soda. With pastry blender (two knives work well) cut in margarine-butter until mixture resembles coarse meal. Mix in the walnuts (HOLD 2 tablespoonfuls aside) and the raisins, then mix in the buttermilk with a fork. Dough will start to pull away readily from side of bowl. Gather the dough into a ball on lightly floured board (flour your hands, too). Then pat dough into a circle about 3/4 inch thick. Cut in half with a sharp knife and then cut each half into quarters. Place on greased cookie sheet. Brush tops with buttermilk and sprinkle with remaining two tablespoonfuls of chopped walnuts. Bake in pre-heated 425 degree OVEN ABOUT 15 MINUTES OR UNTIL NICELY BROWNED. Serve warm for breakfast or any other time of the day (or night!) with butter and marmalade or jam. FABULOUS!

* If you don't have buttermilk, add 1 tablespoonful white vinegar to 3/4 cup low fat milk.

if you like blintzes, you'll love kay's souffle!

Ingredients:

2 packages frozen
blintzes (6 per
pkg.) Use
cheese, cherry
or blueberry
blintzes

1/4 cup marga-
rine

1 1/2 cup sour
half and half
cream (I sim-
plify it and use
1 full pint)

4 eggs, beaten

2 tablespoonfuls
sugar

1 teaspoonful
vanilla

Melt margarine in a 9" x 11" oblong pan. (Place in oven briefly while it is preheating). Place frozen blintzes, 4 to a row in 3 rows on top of melted margarine. In medium or large bowl, beat the eggs; add sour half and half cream, sugar and vanilla and blend. Pour over blintzes. Sprinkle with wheat germ or corn flake crumbs (optional) and bake one hour in preheated 350 degree OVEN or til nicely browned. Serve immediately for a terrific brunch! Serves 6 (two per person). To enhance the serving for a lavish brunch, serve with sour half and half cream, a bowl of cottage cheese, chilled sliced peaches (from a large can) or one pint of sliced, hulled and sweetened fresh strawberries, hot biscuits with butter and jam and plenty of hot coffee. A warmed coffee cake (from the bakery) is a great finale!

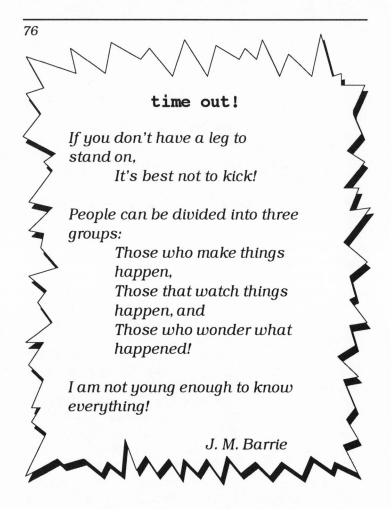

time out!

If you don't have a leg to stand on,
        It's best not to kick!

People can be divided into three groups:
        Those who make things happen,
        Those that watch things happen, and
        Those who wonder what happened!

I am not young enough to know everything!

                                        J. M. Barrie

CONSIDER

American consumers and industry throw away enough aluminum to rebuild our entire commercial air fleet every three months.

Americans go through 2.5 million plastic bottles every <u>hour</u>, only a small percentage of which are now recycled.

spicy kay's chili chowder!

Ingredients:

1 large onion,
chopped (about
1 1/2 cups)
2 tablespoonfuls
corn oil (Author
Canola)
1 green pepper
1 can (16 ozs)
kidney beans,
drained
1 can (15 ozs)
pinto beans,
drained
1 can (15 ounces)
black beans,
drained
2 cans (14 ozs
each) canned,
crushed toma-
toes, undrained
1 can (15 ounces)
chicken broth
3/4 cup picante
sauce (mild,
medium or hot)
1/2 teaspoonful
salt
1 or 2 teaspoon-
fuls tabasco
sauce (or any
hot pepper
sauce)
1 teaspoonful chili
powder,
(medium or HOT)

Cook onion in oil in large Dutch Oven until onion is tender but not brown. Add remaining ingredients EXCEPT optional garnishes. Bring to a boil then reduce heat and simmer 10 minutes (or longer). Ladle into soup bowls and serve with your choice of garnishes (OR without). Serves 8. I suggest serving it with fresh, fat slices of pumpernickel bread. It's spicy!! Even better the next day....IF YOU CAN WAIT THAT LONG!

Optional garnishes:
chopped onions, shredded cheddar cheese, sliced green onions, sour cream.

kay's—
sassy, spicy chicken

Ingredients:

3 lbs. chicken
thighs, skinned
OR 3 lbs. chicken
pieces, skinned
3 tablespoonfuls
margarine
2 tablespoonfuls
Oriental sesame
oil
1 teaspoonful dry
mustard
1 tablespoonful
sesame seeds
1 tablespoonful
cider vinegar
2 teaspoonfuls
low sodium soy
sauce
1 teaspoonful hot
pepper sauce
1 garlic clove,
crushed

Preheat oven to 350°. Place chicken in 13x9x2 (or thereabouts) baking pan. In a small sauce pan, mix margarine, sesame oil, sesame seeds, vinegar, soy sauce, hot sauce, mustard and garlic. Cook over medium heat until butter melts, then lower heat and cook for 4 to 5 minutes. Brush 1/2 of sauce on chicken and bake uncovered for 30 minutes in preheated oven. Turn chicken over and brush with remaining sauce and bake 30 more minutes or until nicely browned and tender. Serves 4. Serve with brown rice (and you can ladle some of this great sauce on the brown rice).

IF YOU HAVE MORE THAN 3 LBS OF CHICKEN, don't worry . . there's plenty of sauce to cover. You'll get complements on this one!

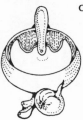

potato salad–
by goring!

Serves 8:

Ingredients:

4 large Idaho
   potatoes
4 hard boiled eggs
   - chopped
1 green pepper -
   cut into small
   pieces
1 large white
   onion - cut into
   small pieces
1 cucumber - cut
   into small pieces
Mayonnaise (non
   cholesterol)
   about 1/2 cup

Boil the potatoes whole, unpeeled (retains the potato flavor). Then cool and take the skin off (very easy). Cut up into appropriate size pieces (1" cube?) and add all of the ingredients listed above. Salt and pepper to taste. Chill before serving. Easy? Add cold cuts to the platter and you have a light supper for yourself and an appreciative date!

. . . . another easy one from Laurie Goring!

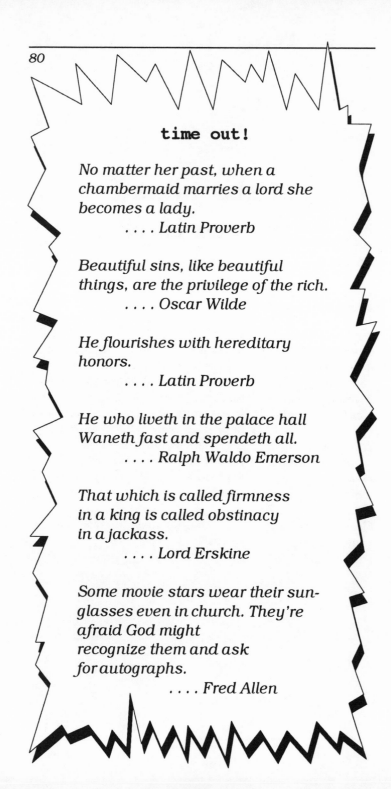

time out!

*No matter her past, when a
chambermaid marries a lord she
becomes a lady.*
          . . . . Latin Proverb

*Beautiful sins, like beautiful
things, are the privilege of the rich.*
          . . . . Oscar Wilde

*He flourishes with hereditary
honors.*
          . . . . Latin Proverb

*He who liveth in the palace hall
Waneth fast and spendeth all.*
          . . . . Ralph Waldo Emerson

*That which is called firmness
in a king is called obstinacy
in a jackass.*
          . . . . Lord Erskine

*Some movie stars wear their sun-
glasses even in church. They're
afraid God might
recognize them and ask
for autographs.*
          . . . . Fred Allen

steamed marinated chicken
-by kay, by ben, "by george"

Ingredients:

1 fryer 2 1/2 lbs
   cut up
1/2 cup lemon
   juice
1 teaspoonful
   Worcestershire
   sauce
1/2 teaspoonful
   garlic salt
1/2 teaspoonful
   seasoned salt
   (Lawry's)
1/4 teaspoonful
   Accent
1/2 teaspoonful
   paprika
1/2 teaspoonful
   salt
1/4 teaspoonful
   black pepper
3/4 cup chicken
   broth
1 tablespoonful
   cornstarch
2 tablespoonfuls
   water or wine
Chopped chives

Put chicken pieces in shallow dish. Mix all ingredients except cornstarch, water or wine, and chives. Pour over chicken and let stand in refrigerator several hours or overnight, turning chicken once or twice. Put in skillet with marinade. Bring to a boil, cover and steam over low heat 1 hour or until tender. Remove chicken pieces to a platter and thicken the liquid with cornstarch blended with water (or wine). Pour sauce over the chicken and sprinkle with chives. Makes 4 servings. Wunderbar!

time out!

"In nine out of ten cases, a woman had better show more affection than she feels!"
. . . . Jane Austin

"I'm living so far beyond my income that we may almost be said to be living apart."
. . . . E. E. Cummings

"A miser is a person who lives within his income. He is also called a magician."

It is impossible to overdo luxury."
. . . . French Proverb

"There is no such thing as justice - in or out of court!"
. . . . Clarence Darrow

"[Fox hunting is] the unspeakable in full pursuit of the uneatable."

. . . . Oscar Wilde

"Niagara Falls must be one of the earliest, and keenest, disappointments in American married life!"
. . . . Oscar Wilde

gloria's apple cake —by mary!

Ingredients:

1 cup sugar
1/2 cup butter or margarine
1 egg
1/2 cup cold, black coffee with 1 teaspoonful baking soda
1 1/2 cup all purpose flour
1 teaspoonful nutmeg
1 teaspoonful cinnamon
1/4 teaspoonful cloves
1/2 cup nuts, chopped
1 cup raw apples, diced (peeled or unpeeled, your choice!)

Mix will the butter/margarine with sugar by using a knife to keep cutting in the sugar (this is called "creaming" - I don't know why! - and you can buy an inexpensive hand device for this purpose at any grocery store); blend in egg and cold coffee with baking soda. Set aside. Sift flour with spices several times. Add flour, apples and nuts to butter mixture. Beat about 2 minutes. Pour batter into greased cake pan (8x8 or if doubling recipe, 9x13) and bake for 1 hour at 325°. Let cake cool in pan for 15 minutes then slide a sharp knife around perimeter of cake, turn over on cake rack and it should slip right out!

Icing:

1/2 cup brown sugar,
4 tablespoonfuls butter
3 tablespoonfuls milk.
1 cup confectioners sugar

Boil for 5 minutes. Blend well. Let stand until cool, then add 1 cup confectioner's sugar. Frost cooled cake.

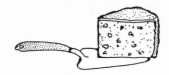

perfect pumpkin pie!

Ingredients:

4 *egg whites*
1 *can (16 ounces)*
  solid-pack
  pumpkin
1/2 *cup honey*
1 *teaspoonful*
  cinnamon
1/4 *teaspoonful*
  cloves
1 2/3 (13 ounces)
  evaporated milk
9 *inch unbaked*
  pie shell with
  high fluted
  edges

Pre-heat oven to 425°. Mix filling ingredients in order given. Pour into pie shell and bake at 425° for 15 minutes. Reduce heat to 350° and continue baking for another 45 minutes or until a knife inserted near the center comes out clean.

Cool completely on wire rack.

KAY'S QUICKIE TIDBIT!

BAKE A BUNDT CAKE PER RECIPE ON BOX. Cool 15 minutes, remove from pan. Pierce top and upper sides with an ice pick and spoon carefully (with a spoon) over the cake and especially into the holes rum or Amaretto or Grand Marnier or whatever your favorite alcoholic beverage is, and let the cake rest for at least 3 hours.

It will be the "bestest" homemade cake you ever ate! You can embellish the cake with slightly toasted almond slices stuck in the ice pick holes!!

dessert without guilt

-or-
non-fat chocolate syrup!!!

From: *Cholesterol & Children: A Parent's Guide to Giving Children a Future Free of Heart Disease* by Robert E. Kowalski. I picked up this recipe at my cardiologist's office!

Blend 1/2 cup of cocoa with 2/3 cup light corn syrup. For a lighter, sweeter syrup, increase corn syrup to one cup.

(Author: Use your imagination with this one to make delightful, easy and quick desserts: spoon over angel food cake, fresh strawberries, or ice cream, or . . well, you get the idea!)

time out!

A crop won't wait until you feel like bringing it in!

Some are bent with toil, and some get crooked trying to avoid it!

The time to relax is when you don't have time for it.
                    Sidney J. Harris

Tomorrow is often the busiest day of the year!

                    Spanish Proverb

some light dips

dijon vinaigrette

Ingredients:

1/4 cup Dijon
Mustard
3 tablespoonfuls
red vinegar
3 tablespoonfuls
soft tofu
1 tablespoonful
white vinegar
1 tablespoonful
onion, chopped
2 cloves garlic,
chopped
1/2 teaspoonful
basil
Pepper to taste
2 drops hot sauce

Combine and blend. Use on pasta, salad or cold slaw. Great over steamed vegetables.

BASIL

spinach dip:

Ingredients:

1 cup chopped,
fresh spinach
1 cup nonfat
cottage cheese
1/2 cup chopped
green onions
1/2 cup nonfat
yogurt
1 tablespoonful
soy sauce
1 clove garlic,
chopped

Blend in the blender and chill.

low-cal tuna or crab dip:

Ingredients:

8 ounces light
  cream cheese
2 tablespoonfuls
  nonfat yogurt
2 teaspoonfuls
  horseradish
2 drops hot sauce
2 dashes
  Worcestershire
  sauce
1/4 cup diced green
  onion
1/4 cup diced celery
1/4 cup green diced
  pepper
6 ounces tuna or
  crab meat
Paprika to taste

Combine and chill well.

deviled dip:

Ingredients:

8 ounces nonfat
  yogurt
2 teaspoonfuls
  mustard
2 teaspoonfuls
  salsa
2 teaspoonfuls
  green diced
  pepper
1/8 teaspoonful
  garlic powder
2 drops hot sauce

Combine well and chill.

curry dip:

Ingredients:

12 ounces nonfat
   cottage cheese
2 tablespoonfuls
   slim milk
1 teaspoonful
   vinegar
1/3 cup peeled,
   seeded and
   chopped cu-
   cumber
1/2 teaspoonful
   curry powder
1/8 teaspoonful
   garlic powder
1/3 cup minced
   green onion

Blend and chill well.

**TRY USING THE FOLLOWING WITH ANY OF THE
ABOVE DIP RECIPES:**

PITA BREAD

TORTILLAS

VEGETABLES

PRETZELS

FRESH DARK BREAD

PUMPERNICKEL !!!

"counter–culture" cornell bread

A Pat Bird Variation

This makes 3 loaves:

Ingredients:

Mix together in a large bowl:
2 cups oatmeal, uncooked (or other whole grain breakfast cereals)
3 tablespoonfuls salad oil
3 teaspoonfuls salt (low sodium!)
1/3 cup honey
3/4 cup sesame seed
1 cup sunflower seeds
3 cups boiling water

LET COOL. Meanwhile, measure and sift together:
4 cups unbleached bread flour (containing wheat germ, or add 2 tablespoonfuls wheat germ) and 1 cup whole wheat flour
1/2 cup full-fat soy flour
3/4 cup non-fat dry milk
2 packages (or 2 tablespoonfuls) dry active yeast

Stir into the cooled oatmeal mixture (should be 120° to 130°) about half of the flour mix. Beat about 75 strokes or 2 minutes with an electric mixer. Mix in remainder of flour and blend (knead) thoroughly for 5 minutes until dough becomes firm.

Turn out on floured board, using one cup more flour if needed. Knead until dough is smooth and elastic. Place dough in greased container. Grease top lightly and cover with cloth or paper towel. Let rise in a warm place until nearly double in size, about 45 minutes. Punch dough down, fold over the edges and turn upside down to rise another 20 minutes. Turn onto board and divide into 3 parts. Make into smooth tight balls. Cover and let stand 10 minutes. Shape into 3 loaves; place in greased tins;

(continued)

loaf tins should be about 8 by 4 1/2 by 3 inches in size. Grease tops lightly and cover. Let rise until dough is double in size, about 1 hour.

Bake in moderate oven, 350° for about 60 minutes. If the loaves begin to brown in 15 to 20 minutes, reduce the temperature to 325°. Remove the bread from the pans and put on a rack or cloth to cool.

. . .Pat Bird, an effective and thoughtful teacher, was a vital marine biologist during the time I was associated with Mote Marine Laboratory, Sarasota, Florida.

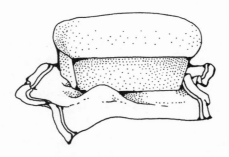

chicken soup

by kay for bud

A few years ago, I was laid low with an unidentified viral infection. Kay Elman made batches of her Chicken Soup which was much more beneficial for me than all the antibiotics in the world! Here's Kay's cure - for YOU! Try it - you'll love it!

Ingredients:

2 pounds chicken necks or chicken backs
3 quarts of water
1 large onion, chopped (or 2 small ones)
1 large carrot, sliced
2 stalks celery, cut into small pieces; include the leaves if you wish
1 bay leaf
1 teaspoonful salt
1 beaten raw egg
1 teaspoonful sour salt (look for this in the Jewish ethnic food section of your supermarket
1/2 teaspoonful thyme
1/2 to 1 teaspoonful black pepper
1/3 cup thin noodles or rice

Remove all pin feathers from chicken pieces and wash in cold water. Place in large pot (5 quart) and add 3 quarts of water. Bring to a boil and then reduce heat to simmer for about 1 hour. Skim off the froth and discard. Add vegetables, bay leaf and regular salt; simmer for another hour. Add 1/3 cup thin noodles or rice and simmer for 15 minutes. Remove chicken pieces and set them aside.

In a medium stainless bowl, beat the egg with a fork. Add sour salt, thyme and black pepper; blend well with a fork. Just before serving, ladle some soup gradually into the egg mixture and pour slowly back into the pot of soup (otherwise, egg will curdle). DO NOT BOIL!

This soup is even better the next day if you can wait that long. Chill overnight in the refrigerator and skim off the congealed fat. Ladle amount to be served into a smaller saucepan and heat until nice and hot. FREEZES VERY WELL!

(continued)

Options:

1. For a main luncheon meal, serve the chicken pieces in the soup, or:
2. For a whopping budget pleaser, pour Kraft barbecue sauce over the chicken pieces and heat in your microwave for 5 minutes. Serve with rice and a big salad and you have a delicious penny-pincher's feast!
3. Use turkey necks or roast turkey carcass (remove when soup is cooked!)
4. Cut up vegetables into large pieces - maybe use 2 large carrots - and blend in osterizer when cooked. This thickens the soup so it is not necessary to add noodles or rice. Serve with dollop of sour cream or garlic croutons!

citrus candy
—by MMH

Here's a recipe given me by dear Mary Mason Hull which recalls some fond memories—we had a nurse during the time my sister had scarlet fever who tickled our palates when she made this confection for all of us. I told Mary about this one day in Costa Rica and here's her recipe:

Cut into thin strips the rind (just the colored outer part) of grapefruit, orange, lime or lemon rind. Soak for 24 hours (refrigerator) in salt water (1 tablespoonful salt per quart of water) using enough salt water to cover all of the peel.

Rinse thoroughly and boil in plain water for 20 minutes. Drain. Cook the peel in a mixture of 1/4 cup water and 1/2 cup sugar. Be careful not to burn the peel (keep shaking the pot), but cook until the peel has absorbed the water-sugar mixture. The peel at this point should be fairly transparent.

Drain thoroughly and roll the cooked, candied peel in either table sugar or confectioner's sugar. Refrigerate.

CONSIDER

He was born in 1735 in Massachusetts. Every student knows his name and can recite the illustrious deed he performed in 1775 during the Revolution. What is not so well known is that he was one of the world's great metal craftsmen and artisans, a pioneer manufacturer and industrialist. In 1801 he founded a major American company that is still alive and thriving today. The company is Revere Copper and Brass, Inc., and the founder was, of course, Paul Revere.

The most important product that America has been able to produce is not the automobile or television or the computer. It is *hope* - hope not only for ourselves but for the world.

If you have your sight, you are blessed. If you have insight, you are a thousand times blessed.

Most of us will never do great things, but we can do small things in a great way.

last word!!

from your veterinarian -

the author!

When the American husband gets as much appreciative fuss made over him (for providing food, shelter, clothes and education for the family) - - as the family dog gets for bringing in the morning newspaper . . . . there will be fewer divorces!

AND . . ONE MORE LAST WORD!!

No man ever lost the fight because he was knocked down . . . he lost because he didn't get up!

And more wisdom - from Jonathan Swift, "May you <u>live</u> all the days of your life!"

AND . . FINALLY!!!

"Today is the tomorrow we worried about yesterday and . . . all is well!"

. . . taught me by my loving Grandmother when I was young and lucky enough to be on her caring knee.

INDEX

APPETIZERS

Bulgarian Eggplant Dip 70
Crab Dip 87
Curry Dip 88
Deviled Dip 87
Dijon Vinaigrette 86
Easy Hors d'oeuvres 8
Garbanzo Bean Dip 72
Party Dip, A Snap 30
Pecan Cheese Ball 25
Spinach Dip 86
Tuna Dip 87
Walnut Chopped Liver 65

BRUNCHES

Blintzes, Kay's Souffle 75
French Toast, Orange Cinnamon 47

SOUPS

Bean (Twelve) Soup 73
Chicken Soup, by Kay 91
Chili Chowder 77
Eggplant Soup 29
French Onion Soup 9
Split Pea Soup 18
Tomato Soup, ala Ambrosia 57

SALADS and DRESSINGS

Potato Salad, by Goring 79
Salad, by Mary 62
Salad Dressing Supreme 17

ENTREES

Beef Dishes

End of Month Meal 34
Hamburger, A Jogger's 42
London Broil 43
Meat Balls, by Joyce 48
Meat Sauce, by Joyce 49
Pot Roast Delicioso 25

Fish Dishes

Mahi Mahi Filet Dijonaise 14
Salmon Filet Dijonaise 14
Susan's Swift Savory Supper 43

Pasta Dishes and Tomato Sauces

Fettucini 42
Italian Tomato Sauce 4
Manicotti, by Henry! 6
Marinara Sauce, ala Suglia 36
One Dish Pasta Delight 40
Pasta with Garlic 71
Spaghetti Sauce by the Two's 38

Poultry Dishes

Baked Chicken 7
Chicken Divan Extraordinare 27
Chicken, "Hull" of 56
Gabriella's Great Chicken Delight 61
"O" Chicken Shish-Kabob 32
Sassy, Spicy Chicken 78
Steamed Marinated Chicken 81
Turkey Loaf 15

Quiche, by Vitrier 12

WOK COOKING 21

VEGETABLES

Beans, Baked Southern Style 19
Carrots, Baked 23
Eggplant, Tasty Parmesan 45
Microwave Vegetables 16
Potato, Baked 35
Potato, Mashed 64
Ratatouille Vitrier 54
Spinach, you'll love it! 20
Squash, Oriental 31

BREADS

Beer Bread, by Joni, By Kay! 72
Cornell Bread, "Counter-Culture" 89
Garlic Sticks 59
Scones, Super Scotch 74

DESSERTS

Apple Cake, Gloria's - by Mary 83
Bundt Cake, Kay's Quickie Tidbit 84
Cheesecake, Susie's 44
Chocolate Syrup, non-fat! 85
Coconut Pie, Super-Easy, by Kay 67
Easy As Pie 33
Hawaiian Cake, from Heaven 63
Perfect Pumpkin Pie 84
Wackie Cake, by Mary 69

CANDIES

Citrus Candy, by Mary 92
Peanut Brittle 64

MISCELLANEOUS

Breast Anatomy 26
Cleaning Copper Bottoms 52
Cleaning Hints 10

Freezing Hints 7
Garlic Press, by "Suzi" 37
Kitchen Equipment 51
Kitchen "Tips" - by Hull 58
"Season To Taste" 13

Here's YOUR Page!

A practical cookbook is one that has a blank page in the back - where you list the phone numbers of the nearest delicatessens, fast food establishments and the like: